BREAD AND BLOOD TONICS

Poems of
UBAKA LEO OGBOGU

PublishAmerica
Baltimore

© 2004 by Ubaka Leo Ogbogu.
All rights reserved. No part of this book may be reproduced, stored in a retrieval system or transmitted in any form or by any means without the prior written permission of the publishers, except by a reviewer who may quote brief passages in a review to be printed in a newspaper, magazine or journal.

First printing

ISBN: 1-4137-5020-6
PUBLISHED BY PUBLISHAMERICA, LLLP
www.publishamerica.com
Baltimore

Printed in the United States of America

dedication

for my family
and Gift, my love

contents

book one forerunner
11	tomorrow morning/
12	my town aged and unkempt/
13	the daughters of Charity have/
14	to be ordinary/
15	church is the right or wrong path/
16	eager to reach the peak/
17	candle beam casts a glow/
18	and they brought forth his cadaver/
19	Sequence/
20	a flash of lightning/
21	idle tools for perversion/
22	Sudan/
23	preacher on a podium prophesies/
24	scented decay from the remains/
25	notice that

the difference in the spelling of regimen and regiment is t. thus the t/

book two songs
29	minuet/
30	cradle song/
31	andante in a minor/
32	dead march/
33	overture/
34	medley/
37	sonata/

book three sequences (or poem 23 or ode to july and timipere)
41	a/
42	b/
43	c/
44	d/
45	e/
46	f/
47	g/
48	h/
49	i/
50	j/
51	k/
52	l/
53	m/
54	n/
55	o/
56	p, q, r/
58	s/
59	t/
60	u/
61	v/
62	w/
63	x/
64	y/
65	z/

book four gift of golden light
69	little elf/
70	ides of June/
71	unplugged/
72	becoming you/
73	antiphon/
74	I opened the door from the dark/
75	dancer/
76	yang/
77	11:50 pm/

book five threnody
81	eunice/
85	patrick/
87	iyawo/
89	no new song/

book six desecration
93	state of the nation/
94	a nursery rhyme for patriots/
96	love/
97	me & HIM/
98	pain/
99	chukwudi/
100	dusk/
102	dawn/
103	the odunlade choir of the church of the resurrected lord/
104	acromegalic/
105	old clock strikes beast hour/
106	ashawo/
107	bundu/

book seven celestial point
111	haiku/
112	après tu le deluge/
113	kaleidoscope/
114	blood unshackles itself/
115	Emmett Till/
116	epitaph/

**book one
forerunner**

1

tomorrow morning
I am sending you a vial of my love
mixed with the strongest poisons
you will die loving me

2

my town aged and unkempt
Rheumatic
yesterday the MANR building
fell flat on its face
in the bitter storm
our chairman's drunken phallus
was in his mistress
grinding mercilessly to the beat of the rain

3

the daughters of Charity have
a brand new bus
town to town they tour
helping the poor appreciate the beauty
of a brand new bus

4

to be ordinary
the cactus grows thorns

5

church is the right or wrong path
so Sunday I sit and stare at
sleek gals in miniskirts
I have chosen the wrong path

6

eager to reach the peak
we trek backward
our hearts in rucksacks
our faces smeared
with the future

our sunglasses
shield our eyes from the glare
of bright future

7

candle beam casts a glow
on brown shadows
inks of light smeared around the moon

four bodies lie on mattresses
breathing softly
as midnight
rushes towards day

snores
spoken as a scream

tomorrow approaches
bringing disjoints
petals falling
off an old tree

8

and they brought forth his cadaver
I gazed upon his anus
it smelt so bad
how can a dead man's anus smell so bad
why must a dead man's anus smell so bad and so forth

then I saw six heads, six tails, six dragons
six oversexed virgins, six, six, six

why must a dead man's anus smell so bad

hear ye
to each that can smell
he did not die in the loo

9

Sequence

do you fear consequence

10

a flash of lightning
shatters the skull of night
spreading its balmy membranes
to the cruelty of thunder

I jolt in my sleep
hurriedly grabbing at my shadows
as a drowning man clutches at the river's surface
to exit myself
and the tortuous rhythms of death
playing Pilate with my soul
washing its hands of my infested blood

I have dragged my cross to too many crucifixions
returning three days later
to mock the misery of biblical follies

but why do I still fear the night

11

idle tools for perversion
biros stuck in our pinnas
lice scratchers

flotsam
we jog the streets
searching for rotten bread
to feed
brain famine

12

Sudan
American manna drops
says my promiscuous radio
human opportunity cost born
the weakest hung out to die
in the sun
the weak be obliged
mother make your choice

13

preacher on a podium prophesies
the apocalist is drawn
sceptre and crown tumbles down
in its place reigns
the arrogance of silence

it came to pass
on many a fortnight away
he tumbles away and down
herald to his passing word

a word made flesh
dwelling among the putrid and putrefactions

in his place reigns
the poor crooked sceptre and crown

14

scented decay from the remains
of abacha's soul

Passover time, dear lord
we have smeared our lintel with his blood
saviour do not pass us by

15

    notice that the difference in the spelling of regimen and regiment is t. thus the t when fully crossed after the dotted i transforms a life promoting word into a unit of human batteries used for crushing life. which is why the word gun can be used to kill a gnu because the u has taken the place of the n in the semantic order. attempts to explain this phenomenal boisterousness of the English language will essentially culminate in futility or headaches. fodamore god is spelt in two ways one with a small letter g and the other with a capital letter g to explain nuances and the African one and blood is the same every place whether in America or Accra or in the dictionary or spilled in Somalia or is donated transfused drunk or used to manufacture bread and blood tonics.

book two
songs

16

minuet

to fathom the beauty
of a chameleon
is mere fantasy

17

cradle song

beneath every grey strand
a sea of problems

eyes sketching solutions in the noisy vacuum
of the classroom

across the room
his blood picks up her gallant buttocks
swoosh swoosh to the boy bonking her

18

andante in a minor

lover's snapshot
carefully brutalized
whip scars on my back

family values on a Kodak paper
chastised by rats at the edges
price for time together

colourful smiles
fade from paper
love palms grasped as clothesline
to dry secret tears
wills
worn
in dimple pits on each cheek

stranded in dumb speech
eyes seeing only its blindness

19

dead march

shots shatter in the heat
fragments lacerate your earlobes
your gun falls your deafness deepens
the blood drips down your fatigues crimson
tickles your tears you grab your scrotum
you scream your scrotum swells
your voice cracks your oesophagus swells

the kwashiorkor kid
you
mothershot
awaits American manna
flesh clutches ribs for life
head heavy hot and swollen

20

overture

up up gold hill
spice heart turns to stone
unto the ladderbottomer's sill
scorn sputum on spare bone

vanity of vanities
vernal passing fancies
what man's fantasy
wins paradise's odyssey

21

medley

dawn
wandering feelings
sink with the crow of the cock
the Fall

carcasses of pain
sculpted on my mind's joy
like fauna on palm

the carcass of my joy

pumpkin
the more I grow
the more I die

epileptic foaming
licking the froth
of tangent-packed saliva
breaking words
drowning hearts
we circle around resolution
finding none
at the delta
thunderbolts race as semen
fuses with blood in hot copulation

circles round resolution
finding none
we batter
our bounty
with the stony silence of ignorant gods
man and made
all sides shattered

seduced split side
anger in my foul head
onion peels in my feelings
tears camouflaged as blood
shadows creep
beneath the glow of the deserted moon playground
stealing substantial songs
life mirage on *Oko* road
fade before fathom
welcome to New Year's Eve
my nostrils
mothersucked to life
welcome to
my rise from grace to grass

night I am the foetus
do not touch the door
or my ghost will greet
night
my head rests on paper mats
my dreams give violent chase
night
mosquito cries mate with slaps
my mind mingles with the blood

bothered
a tiny footpath crisscrossed

by infrared spider webs
a mound of faeces
my bonafide spectacles pop
such human benevolence
bothered
seriously thinking of nothing
through sun moon and blasphemy
I have ventured
slung my heart in a pouch
bled internally
arose
three exaggerated days after
a colossal clown

so I am sick of nothing
nothing
eating up my big head

so I swore one early dawn
when the shitty head cock in our yard
screamed a new day
wrapped in old garments
I swore never again
to write profanities

but I am sick of nothing
eating up my big head
last night I met Jesus
just before I met that vain prostitute
begging me for sex in my dreams
IN MY DREAMS

22

sonata

propelling you
through dream and space
she assumes a body of light
like a shooting star

no more will she be
a memory
of a daydream

a conjurer's stick brings her to life
today

book three
sequences
(or poem 23 or ode to July and timipere)
a to z of life. same days and lonely nights and the mind travels like a chugging train...

a

July
month of my birth
brings me renewal
I am reborn
a mutated make carving out
the present from the past

in the throbbing of my temples
imbalance regurgitates its passion
in the soaring of velvet hopes
soft confusion then dementia
and insomnia brew

b

yesterday I wove a cloak of fear
with a mask and two eyeholes
to see the world better

I saw a lot of upturned faces
sugar faces
pale telltale faces
faces of gold
faces of sold

c

the fly gauze shutter
artwork of graph-like gauze and recreating flies
within never without
keeping in the flies

d

do not let this trail of thought
leave my sunken head bitch
success is a woman's face
an eternal task to keep away wrinkles

e

anxious faces in the buttery
we beg for plenty
in the midst of plenty

f

I look at your face noliwe
and miss a distant face

g

possum o possum
he loves to straddle you
thighs over muscle
bleeding his tears off your juices

h

detonating bombs
we test strength
starving babies to death
we lead
making pills to raise penises from the dead
we advance scientifically

i

preface of a song of desire
plays out an ancient chorus
in white faced morning
shadows saunter soullessly
distinct as silhouettes
staring at blind backs
plucking at dregs of conscience

j

hung my sorrows close to your ears
and you wept
did not come to you for lack of tears
this mockery of my misery

k

thrust
morning into a new day

venerated Iscariot
born of a dual implosion

1

your heart desires it
your heart cannot achieve it
for fear of breaking your heart

m

boy and girl
so much in love
hate each other so
they fought and fought
girl thinks I should leave
lucid post eruption
she searches for
remains of ruins strewn
over motherland

n

adventures in flirting
with you my dear Bimbo
has deepened my resolve
to try not to achieve
what can be achieved

o

countless ways I can love you
countless ways I can leave you
so seek not virgin promises from me
my heart is a small splash of saliva
left neatly on a wet pavement

p, q, r

in the second epiphany
we ventured from a land of wisdom
arid in love
with strands of flipsided grey
we calmed the flames within
with tomorrow

tomorrow of the beautiful eyes
tomorrow of the comely smile
tomorrow of our satin dreams
we left
a maddened magi
we saw a southern star
twinkling near the sun
we left
seeking reunion with love
love the touch of a mother
love the thighs of a friend
we left

beside you
and the rivers of your feminine grace
that touch of turquoise
the sea bellies midway
driven in smooth ripples
like aerated silk
I squat

taunted by the fool's rush of waves
flinging its body in supplication
at my fears

she would always emerge
in charismatic progressions
through two metre footways
her watery steps studded with my metaphors

beside you
a million tests
I search for fury
and find gales
I look for holes
and find gateways
hands and tongues
these feel like manacles
I try hard to fail
and pass woefully

she would ever shatter
the strain of lowliness
a true queen
a salve for her own sores

s

gravitating in space
mind vacuum a soul solitude
electric nothingness
ohms of reeling images
czar
elevation above denigration
going mad
broken vista in the rising sun
rising retard
songbird
darkness
car visual motion of life
paranoid lust for concentration
mole
all black and under feet
trod on but stuck on the world

                              t

           from where comes help

u

I am in love
with something/someone I cannot identify

v

shadow worshipper
doomed by ungodly desires
sun-ignore spittle
wetness nauseating
sorrow initiate
shrunk before fear

w

have you ever thought of dying young
to leave to the world a beautiful corpse
free of wrinkles
shorn of scorn

X

splash of stillness
time made flesh
twist of memory
knock on the head
termite travels through clay highways
on the courtroom wall
crashed by the briskness of a broom
mole on my thigh
seeking for eyes
hidden by modesty
jug full of water
thirst for bite
maiden's lacerated earlobes
craving for gold
whisper in the dark
no light to guide me there
touch my grey hair
and tell me how much longer
I have to live

y

July, your beauty is now a memory
some old moonlight night in my childhood
a small stroke of cold
an elder's awesome voice
cracked like the groan from the oesophagus
of an old transistor
tragedy or comedy
dream or nightmare
dawn or dusk

the theme of this haphazard poem
the pages of my life

z

elegy to you
Eunice
you will die
dear death
waiting for me to die

**book four
gift of golden light**

24

little elf

nightfall we christened the footpath
with light footsteps and little talk
in your eyes, comets blazed
your hair sparkled like overfed stars
I stood on tiptoe
plucked an astral ribbon from the moon
tied it to the shortest braid
then gazed as erophobic aliens
kissed the moon dust
when my kiss like buoyant satellites
landed on your cheek
Gagarin has landed on godland
cosmic dust and rocky glades
russet flora and nor'easters
herald the event
as I stepped sweetly unto your heart

25

ides of June

on the ides of June
I will strike your windowpane
do not Caeser
I have come to take you

far to a place
where I can stroke your satin cheeks gently
as a knife caresses the face of butter

far to a place
where I will not dream of your face
but face the dream that is you

26

unplugged

misty morning
walk in
I am the mist waiting to embrace you

Scorching sun
search for my laughter
to canopy your flagellation

dim dusk
lay the day to sleep
I am the night forging your every dream in gold

27

becoming you

double dosage of love elixir
you or nothing

28

antiphon

behold in the eyes of the beholder
the beheld

earth brings desire

a beholding

29

I opened the door from the dark
beside the triangular beam of light
you stood, my gift of golden light

30

dancer

head moulding smiles with
mushroom hair packed in shiny *ude aku* split paths
like Benin highway hued with mirage
silver rivulets body contouring
light and brittle
drumsticks in mid action
tanned bronze by the tropical sun
legs shuffle feather orbs swooshing
to digested cuds of ageless rhythms
refreshed by the boom of the *Udu* and *Ibome*
turning and twisting like kosotops spun
from expert fingers
swirling spinning in the brown sand
burrowing furrowing up a dust fog like
Sahara sandstorms
stretching expanding like oil painting set in Fulani
shaking jiggling
ayolo screaming on feet and waist
musical chair pause
abstract art on mansion walls

31

yang

I shine because of you
no longer changing
I rest my heart with you

32

11:50 pm

bond in vacuum
linking souls telephonically
I touch your face
tracing dots around your love
eyes

bliss gone merges heaven now

when you are away
I see you more

**book five
threnody**

33

eunice

i

we cleared the debris from the room
dragging our footsteps
away from the deeps
we tried to think
yet thought only of trying
not to think

we stumbled on heaps of dust
falling hard on our tears
into tiny fragments our minds broke
and we tried to touch
the things we could no longer touch

pain
an octave higher than love

a cracked cry
a fallen rain
a distinguished ache
the vanity of a boomerang

this ribbon of cold
wrapped around me
some salvation or simple surrender

every now and then
some violent memory
comes rushing in
like a fever blast

weeping I embrace
the demons
thoughts drum hard on the heart

each morning sires mourning
living feels like leaving

ii

at the brink of golden sunset
chosen for elevation
you leave
and we adorn your memory
with elegant black robes

meet me at the revival
where
cotyledons burst the earth

iii

the heat simmers
under the sun
dryness crackles
in the spit
I find solace in my cracking lips
smearing my tongue
with gorge offerings of bloody saliva

gone up in fumes
shore sallow salt

my soul is the salt of the river

I hate what I will become
I will become what I hate

I must go to church
and drown myself in Hail Marys

I will kiss the night goodbye
and lay awake

I could sabotage my life
blow out its fuse
die an unproven hypothesis
perhaps then I would return
a beautiful girl
or a thorny plant
or a sack of bones
mourning a dis-bodied soul
at the Judgement

if I die
please exhume my soul
before you bury me. amen

iv

across the fields
gleam of growth
tarnished
by arrogant beige sandstorms

                    each blade weeps from
                       the rape of season

                                creeper
                  your tears lie in pustule
                 your roots torn by the trod

34

patrick

your death caresses the cancers in my heart
the soothing scourge of devil bean seeds
tonight
I gather the embers of your memory

when cold winds blow
the backsides of a poet are tickled
he giggles like a naughty girl

gargling giggles guzzled down his throat like the
beautiful wild wailing of a bereaved belle the poet
cries his head as big as the moon that dreamt away
lazily the night before your passage

tonight
I gather the ashes of your fate

the hairpin bends spanning *ubu*
lead us back to the morning
where the moon lies in silent subjugation
as the flesh of a coconut fruit

you grappled the noon headlong
those gruesome ghouls quarried in your soul
and fell flat on your face as a toddler

>   tonight
>   I gather the salve stubs of your cigarette sticks
>   to build your catafalque on the moon
>
>   in the speech filled silence of the night when
>   our eyes mated the sable song of the clouds
>   the cancers in your head sowed your wheat
>   seeds that fell fanatically in the midst of
>   tortuous thorns
>
>   tonight
>   I gather the pages of your tracts and bibles
>   and burn them for Ash Wednesday

35

iyawo

N'dee
I taste your bile
on my pungent palates

at the crossover
I was handed a wet flame
a flame robust with tears
with its sodden ash I made four marks
east west north and south
of your fragile tender heart
and headed northwards

to a land where the rising sun
like a thriving pang of hunger
lingers around my dark innards

N'dee
when your guiding star was flung
like a breath forever into the clouds
your freshly cut umbilical dangled bloodily
in her stiff hands
while we cried our cheeks
battered by tears
you strolled to her side
to await the coming of morning

then I should have led you
to the crimson marks on the tombstone

yet I ignored the moment and headed northwards
to a land where memories blossom like tulips
its shoddy radiance blurring the lacerated picture
of a new dawn

N'dee
tomorrow when you have found answers
may these words be a testimonial of my love for you
little one
when your milk teeth have all found home
in the crevices of our rusty zinc roofing
forgive
or forget me

36

no new song

your harsh wet drums
cleanses Earth's dusty face
your first is furious
novice swimmer
you lust for breath

tomorrow the sparkle of my white slippers
will mock the eyes of dawn

the winds whistles
a house falls
one pawpaw ripens
ritual begets ritual

I met my old lover at dawn
I said to her, "Old things have passed away"
but she smiled
priestess of Obida
and wiped tata's nose

**book six
desecration**

37

state of the nation
dedicated to military rule in Nigeria

dhfsgqhebfuijfjeewq
ufhgyefhoqewiuoii
jkdhfunmxo[>;lm7873
hhbvbnhvoie9889dop90
vcnjduq78r64

hujbugjvikmmkv
nvnfuvjka;;\'-
iaofqo934jgjggjgjjjjg
r9009t930jgkk

qwasedrftgyhujikoopl;lp
////?????????????????

38

a nursery rhyme for patriots

i your commander-mis-chief
i saw a child with big head and sticking out ribs
i said to its mother
i told her with tears in my eyes
woman may god punish you both you and your child
may your child die of kwashiorkor
may your breast dry up and may you both be put
on fish rings and roasted
don't you know my gofment has no money for the poor
i heard a very important talk talk oversabi write write freedom
fighter bullshit man say our environment this our environment that
this one say that one no say
i said may your mother suffer stroke
may your father piss blood
he did not hear i
said don't you know i and my gofmental people must burn the oil
we must scatter scatter the environment
we must pollute your water
kill your fish
for the survival of the nation
for four fillion barrels of oil equal to four something something
fillion dollars per each armed felon ruling councillor's Swiss account
the bastard did not hear
so i bought a noose with the oil money
and hanged him

but i think what about some of this oil money for
the child and mother on fish rings
and i said, "Ah, foolish thinking"

(dedicated to the memory of Ken Saro-Wiwa)

39

love

emasculation is our love
the Nazarene lied about love
his love fossils in our hearts

our love is carnal
of mouths and tasteless organs

40

me & HIM

I read of the Christ of Calvary in a storybook
his passion was to allow himself
the mockery of a peasant's death

dear Christ of the Jews
my gums are full of holes
the holes are full of blood and wafer cadavers

dear Christ of the Jews
pass me your stripes
to whip the world to sense

no Baptist foretold of my coming
to my grumbling father

41

pain

My vision is not blurred
I am just not seeing better

I wish I could stare above and around
and ponder at what my eyes behold

I wish I could sing sonorous songs
on the choked accompaniment of intestinal grunts

thank providence my secret hours
are orange globules sucked dry and protected by peel

thank providence I can silently anger
at thoughts dead fearful of dying
of tears beneath my eyeballs running
violently washing off the salty remains

of my evaporated glee
oblivious to my plea for its scorching feel
on my scorched cheeks

gather the gongs and flutes
this beat is long broken
by the callous laughter

of a melodic drought

42

chukwudi

we were radial willows
with roots that strained to kiss
beneath earth's light eyes
quilting our shoddy rags
with sweet wind rustle song

43

dusk

night came slowly
sighing with the day's worries
the moon
bucked under home going clouds and resurfacing
lay like a gold brooch
full on azure heavens
the panting sun
spread its blinder diameter
like spilled oil paint
expanding into a terra cotta ball
journeys towards azimuth
it whimpers and trembles
a weak smile on its last face
then back flips
like a long jumper
into a yawning horizon
is devoured
at the bus stop
a commuter rush
cripples rise
and walk
the blind see the pathways of darkness
on the sidewalk
a flurry of homebound feet
street hawkers matchmake the tail ends of their lappas

condense on low stools
ready for the night market
the stench of another passing day
mingles with automobile smoke
glowing cigars
crashing hopes

44

dawn

dawn comes quickly
messianic crescendo
thin sheaves of metallic light
pierce
the dusty louvers
the tropical morning breeze
comes through the cracks
sharp asthmatic ebby
grid; pupils interlock
relief is lost with realization
inside mazy
a juxtaposition of options
dimpled by the orchestrating jazz
of domestic life
outside
tropical troubles
shake off inertia
life goes on

45

the odunlade choir of the church of the resurrected lord

>your voices inspire the dying stars
>they glow brighter and brighter
>expanding to fill each tattered space
>on tattered earth
>
>invading sound and light
>mingles with the beat of pleas
>
>tomorrow's daily bread must be baked
>with scarred hands clear eyes and clear vocal cords
>
>I drift slowly to sleep
>making love to your soloist in my sinful dreams

46

acromegalic
your noon face

you came to break the day
strapping misery metals

you fed us with cuds

unwelcome
opthalmia

47

old clock strikes beast hour
marathon desire
set at hexagonal dimensions
hasty
lovers' garments defrocked
strewn in shreds

latitudinal packaging
of golden dermis
streaking
with silvery rivulets of fever

the erect mingles with the deep
bolt and nut interlock
stylistic seesaws
eurhythmics to animal hee-haas

SHATTER

48

ashawo

selling mascara and vagina

at rising prices

49

bundu

it arrives
drumming the *ine* beat on dusty rooftops

accelerates

washes away the night
to reveal a new day

mingling
the siren song of mosquitoes
bearing the hearse of gassed brethren

accelerates

like a sigh escapes breath

lover's tempo in mid throb

pellets of water dance to carnival pitch

flying by my eye

suddenly

it shakes itself dry
hangs out the rainbow to dry
in the rising sun

the mist
like bleached palm oil fumes

watches over

bundu

**book seven
celestial point**

50

haiku

water rots the pane
dead daffodils spring up to cup
winter drops melting

51

après tu le deluge

you lie fallow Okene
in the sun
your dusty hills slumbering beyond the horizon
you slowly open your ancient thighs
to mock they who lick its rustic glory

I have passed land with turquoise skies
rippling with the promise of bounty
lands where fair maidens
carry their amplified buttocks with dignity
beneath lush clothing
elegant as ubulu cockerels

at your doorstep I begged for love
but you rewarded me with the scorching slap
of your dingy intestines

I am on a sojourn to a land far worse
where knowledge is trapped in overhead speakers
and the cadaverous love of modern women

Okene, après tu le deluge
avec toi le deluge

52

kaleidoscope

sitting at the edge of the pit all through
we watched calamities go by
swift as fast car louver images
often we would remember
quiet times
crystal ball histories in luminous globules of tears
deltas of pain across the banks of our cheeks

but they ever so often dry up
leaving behind streaks of salty white hope tossed across our faces
like salaaming Moslems
as we ponder
the back flip of the setting sun
the diamond light of sunrise

53

blood unshackles itself
from the gored tombs of steel bullets
the body
overloaded mammy-wagon on the run
stretches in the dance of ancestral masquerades
and
to the world
offers hot liquid feces
silhouetted against hellish mirage
the disheveled mass of red brains
lies to rest among fellows

54

Emmett Till

time tills the soil
where your shattered face is sown
to bring forth a harvest of misery
dear Emmett
long after this land consumed itself
garnished with the tender sauce of your blood
your brain bits remain lodged in gnashing teeth

55

epitaph

"old roger is dead and gone
to his grave"
hum haa haa haa haa
haa haa aah aah ah

Printed in the United States
24157LVS00001B/49-96